Cutting-Edge STEM

Cutting-Edge
3D Printing

Karen Latchana Kenney

Lerner Publications ◆ Minneapolis

Lerner Publications Company
A division of Lerner Publishing Group, Inc.
241 First Avenue North
Minneapolis, MN 55401 USA

For reading levels and more information, look up this title at www.lernerbooks.com.

Main body text set in Adrianna Regular 14/20.
Typeface provided by Chank.

Library of Congress Cataloging-in-Publication Data

Names: Kenney, Karen Latchana, author.
Title: Cutting-edge 3D printing / by Karen Latchana Kenney.
Description: Minneapolis : Lerner Publications, [2019] | Series: Searchlight book. Cutting-edge STEM | Includes bibliographical references and index.
Identifiers: LCCN 2017047869 (print) | LCCN 2017057665 (ebook) | ISBN 9781541525351 (eb pdf) | ISBN 9781541523463 (lb : alk. paper) | ISBN 9781541527720 (pb : alk. paper)
Subjects: LCSH: Three-dimensional printing—Juvenile literature.
Classification: LCC TS171.95 (ebook) | LCC TS171.95 .K46 2019 (print) | DDC 621.9/88—dc23

LC record available at https://lccn.loc.gov/2017047869

Manufactured in the United States of America
1-44419-34678-2/15/2018

Contents

Chapter 1

WHAT IS 3D PRINTING?

What do pizza, a wrench, an electric guitar, and a human ear have in common? All of them can be printed using 3D printers!

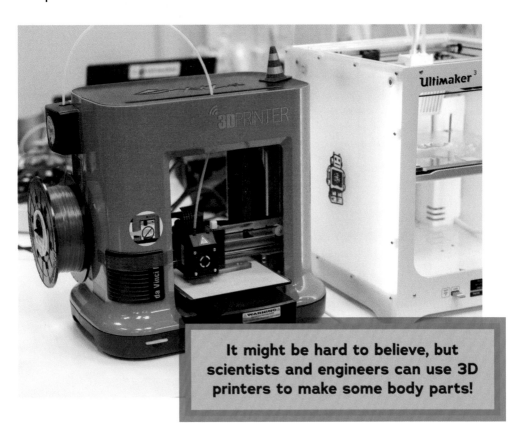

It might be hard to believe, but scientists and engineers can use 3D printers to make some body parts!

Many 3D printers have a platform where the printed object sits during its creation.

A 3D printer prints 3D objects. A 3D object isn't just a shape, like a square that you print on paper. A square is wide and tall. It has two dimensions. A box, though, is a 3D object. It has a square shape, but it has three dimensions: width, height, and depth. You can hold it in your hands.

Design What You Want

Different kinds of 3D printers print different objects. Some print food. Others create pieces of art or fashion, such as vases or jewelry. Some can print human cells to make human tissue. And larger 3D printers have even built houses.

These different 3D-printed objects all begin with a digital design. People use computer programs to design what they want to make. This design becomes printing instructions for the printer. Then the object can be printed.

All of these things were created using 3D printers.

Science Fact or Science Fiction?

Astronauts may soon be able to 3D print pizza in space.

It's a fact!

The National Aeronautics and Space Administration (NASA) asked BeeHex, a Texas company, to develop a 3D printer that prints food. Astronauts would use this technology on missions to other planets in our solar system. BeeHex has already made a printer that prints pizzas. This printer may be used on NASA's upcoming Mars mission, planned for launch sometime in the 2030s.

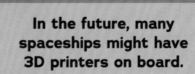

In the future, many spaceships might have 3D printers on board.

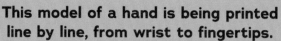

This model of a hand is being printed line by line, from wrist to fingertips.

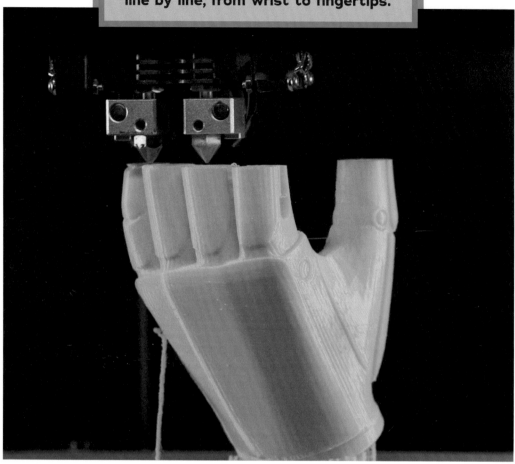

Adding Up the Layers

Just like a regular printer, a 3D printer prints in lines. It uses raw materials, such as a sugar mixture for candy, as its "ink." The printer stacks line upon line of the material on a platform. The lines stick together, and soon they make a solid object.

Within minutes to hours, an idea can become something you can hold. You don't even have to go to a store to buy it. This technology is changing the way people create objects.

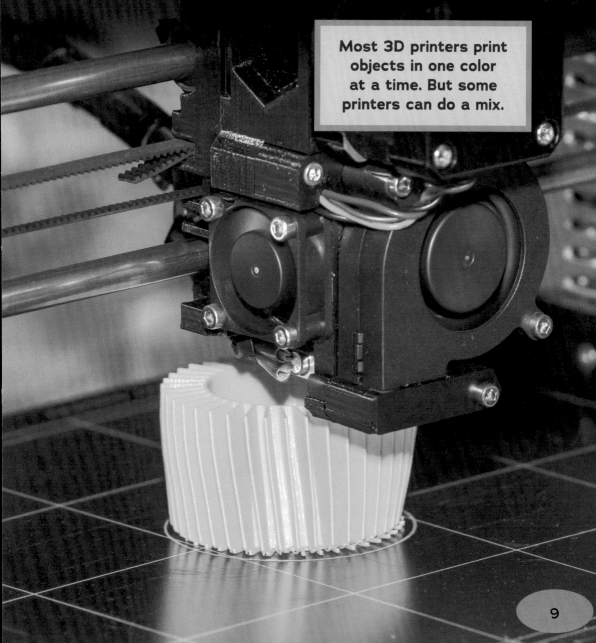

Most 3D printers print objects in one color at a time. But some printers can do a mix.

Chapter 2

HOW 3D PRINTING WORKS

Since its invention by engineer Charles Hull in the 1980s, 3D printing has changed a lot. Hull made models of new machine parts. Workers could test these models, called prototypes, to see if they worked in machines. But making prototypes took several weeks. Hull wanted to print plastic in layers to make the models. He built a machine to do this quickly and cheaply—the 3D printer.

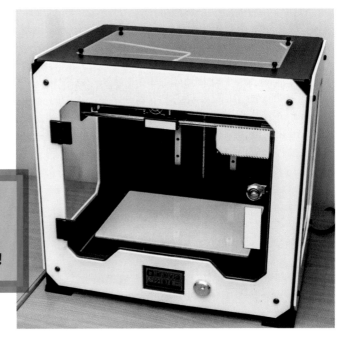

Modern 3D printers can print some objects in just a few minutes!

The material used in 3D printers can make the printers clogged or dirty. Most manufacturers offer cleaning instructions.

For about two decades, only industrial companies used 3D printers. They printed prototypes and machine parts. Now almost anyone can do 3D printing. Whether for personal or industrial use, it begins with an idea and a computer.

Designing a Model

Making a model starts with computer-aided design (CAD), a computer program. With lines and shapes, users can build 3D designs of the objects they want to print. CAD can create a precise drawing of an object. It lets users look at the object from different angles. They can see the top, bottom, and sides. It's quick and easy to change a design in CAD. Once the design is perfect, it can move to the next step.

This CAD drawing will be the model for a 3D-printed object. The designer can see all angles of the project.

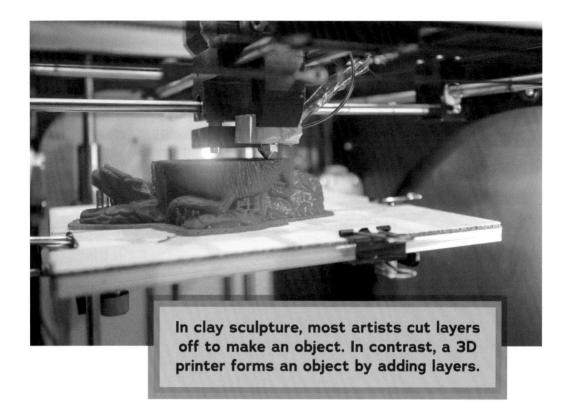

In clay sculpture, most artists cut layers off to make an object. In contrast, a 3D printer forms an object by adding layers.

Slicing It Up

A 3D printer prints by building up many thin layers. It needs instructions on how to make the shape of each layer. But the CAD design shows a whole object. To make the printer understand, a designer uses computer-aided manufacturing (CAM) software. It changes the design into hundreds or thousands of horizontal layers. These CAM instructions tell the printer where to move its printer head, the part of the printer that releases the raw material to make the object. The software also tells the printer when to release materials.

Coding Spotlight

CAM software (*below*) turns a design into a code, or set of instructions, that the printer uses to print. Each line of geometric code, or g-code, instructs the printer to move in a certain way. This line of g-code, for instance, tells the printer to move in a straight line to a certain place on a 3D grid: G1 X6 Y3 Z4. G-code also tells the printer how and when to move its printer head, how much raw material to release, and how fast to release it.

Printing Objects

Next, the printer can build the object. To do this, the printer releases its raw materials from its printer head. Different kinds of 3D printers do this in different ways. Some drop a powder and then a liquid that binds the

powder together. Other printers release a melted material that hardens. The most common 3D printing material is plastic.

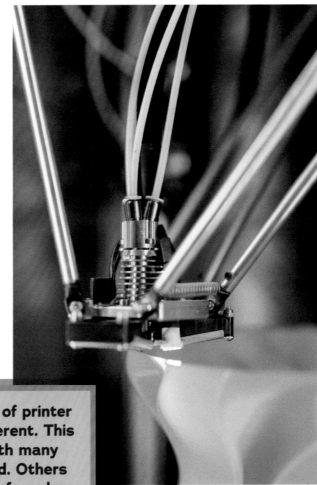

Different kinds of printer heads look different. This one is flat with many tubes attached. Others look more like funnels.

The printer head moves back and forth and up and down over a platform. It makes one layer and then the next. The object slowly builds up until it looks like the design. Then users can touch, use, or even eat the objects they've designed.

Making fancy pancake designs with a 3D printer is more precise than making them on a griddle.

Chapter 3

MAKING PRINTED OBJECTS

For engineers and designers, 3D printing is a quick and cheap way to do their work. If they just need one item, they can make just one. And 3D printing is much faster than traditional manufacturing. Even better, 3D printing uses only the materials it needs. Nothing is wasted, unlike other methods of making objects. Companies still use 3D printing to make prototypes. But now they're making final products too.

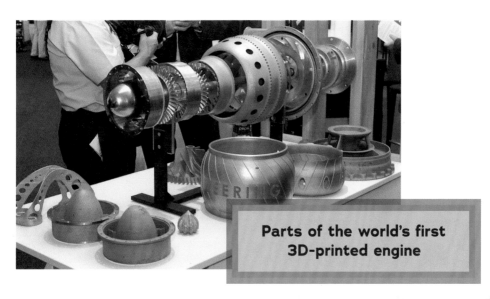

Parts of the world's first 3D-printed engine

Light and Fast Machines

Just zoom in on a Formula One race to see 3D printing in action. At super high speeds, these race cars need to be as light as possible. More weight can mean losing a race. That's why the McLaren Formula One team is 3D printing brake parts and more right from the track. The printers use carbon, a light metal, as part of the printing materials.

ON RACE DAYS, THE MCLAREN MCL32 GETS NEW AND IMPROVED PARTS 3D PRINTED ON-SITE.

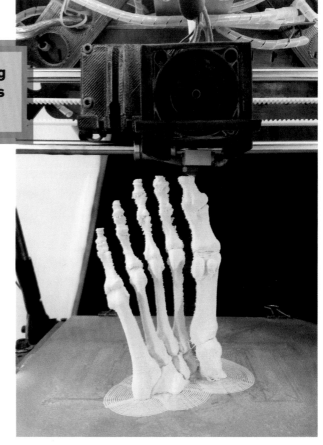

This printer is making a model of the bones in a human foot!

Inside Humans

Picture yourself stepping into an operating room. A team of surgeons has spent months preparing for a complicated operation. They will separate one-year-old twins Jadon and Anias McDonald, who are joined at the head. The two boys share bone, skin, and veins. But by studying a 3D-printed model of their heads, the surgeons know just where to cut. That helps them separate the boys and save their lives. These printers can make models of body parts, such as the twins' heads. They can also print bones and parts of organs.

3D Printing in Action

Researchers have used 3D printing to make human ears. They printed the form of an ear from plastic. Then they injected it with human stem cells. As the form dissolved, the stem cells grew and changed into cartilage. That became a full ear made from human cells. Printed ears could help people with ear injuries. But the researchers developed this ear to help children born with microtia. The disease affects their ears, which never fully develop. This method helps children get new ears.

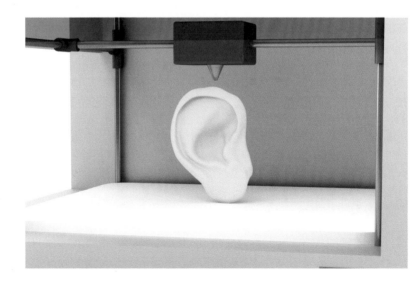

Made for Makers

Imagine you're learning about the Middle Ages in school. The teacher discusses catapults, war machines once used to hurl boulders at walled cities. Then your class gets to design your own catapults. You make CAD designs and print the catapults from a 3D printer.

Anyone can print items, at school or at home, with small 3D printers. People make jewelry, sculptures, tools, and more.

This table and lamp, on display at a 2016 technology conference in Italy, were made by 3D printing.

Chapter 4

WHAT'S NEXT FOR 3D PRINTING?

The future of 3D printing is full of possibilities. It could change industries in big ways. Traditional manufacturing methods still work best for making products in large quantities. But factories use 3D printing if they want to make a small quantity of something. The technology is getting better, though. Soon more and more products will be printed.

Most athletic shoes, including these, are made in large-scale factories in countries around the world.

The AM4LDN running shoe was made at the Speedfactory, a high-tech new factory in Germany.

future factories

Picture this: a steady hum from rows of 3D printers fills the air. No big machines or loud noises at this factory. You're in Ansbach, Germany, where Adidas has a new kind of shoe factory, the Speedfactory. With 3D printing and robots, the factory can make shoes fast. And it will be able to change what it makes quickly. By simply changing a design, the 3D printers can make a new product. Soon customers may be able to order unique shoes.

FORD IS TRYING OUT 3D PRINTERS FOR SOME OF ITS CAR PARTS, SUCH AS THE SPOILER ON A MUSTANG.

Carmakers are looking at 3D printing for their factories too. It will allow them to make custom cars. And it will be a cheaper, faster way to make parts. Ford is already testing 3D printing for large car parts. The printers also make small numbers of other parts and custom items.

Into Space

Next, imagine astronauts on the moon. They're building a base to stay there. But they're not building with their hands. They are printing structures with a 3D printer. It's using moon dust to make domes. That's what the European Space Agency (ESA) hopes to do. It seems possible, but printers have a long way to go before they can build a lunar base.

The ESA is working with architects to test ways of using 3D printers to build housing on the moon.

Astronauts on the International Space Station (ISS) are already using 3D printers for tools and parts. New printers will allow the astronauts who live there to fix broken machines easily. Two new printers in development stand out. They not only 3D print objects. They can also recycle old ones. Materials take a long time to travel to the ISS from Earth. So recycling old materials helps a lot.

Astronauts at the ISS Kibo Laboratory use some 3D-printed tools and parts in their experiments with space medicine, biology, biotechnology, and more.

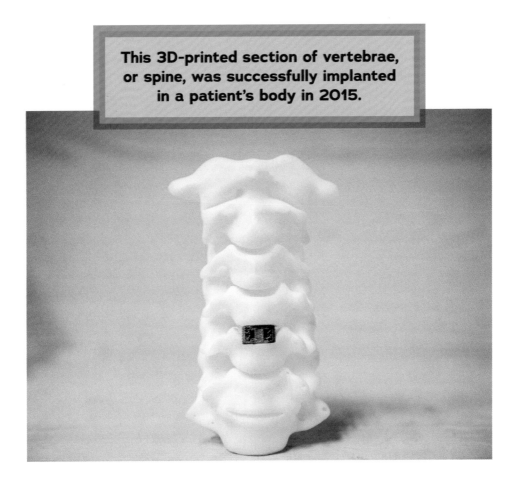

This 3D-printed section of vertebrae, or spine, was successfully implanted in a patient's body in 2015.

New Organs

What if you were very sick and needed a new organ? Instead of waiting months for a donor organ, you could have one printed. Printing organs and body tissues is called bioprinting. Scientists are working on printing organs, but it's difficult. Most organs are complex body parts. So far, scientists have been able to create simpler organs, including bladders. But they hope someday to create complex organs, such as kidneys and hearts.

What else will 3D printing make possible? Scientists and engineers are working to find out. From pizzas to domes on the moon and more, 3D printing's potential seems endless.

Want to design your own electric guitar? It's not cheap, but some people are using 3D printers to make their personalized guitar dreams come true!

Science Fact or Science Fiction?

People can fly inside a 3D-printed airplane.

Not yet! But it may be possible soon.

Airplane maker Airbus is already using printed parts in their planes. They've already made a small drone airplane. Almost every piece was printed. Then the drone was put together from the parts. Airbus hopes to print an entire passenger airplane one day.

In the future, all the parts of an airplane could be created by 3D printers.

Glossary

bioprinting: 3D printing human cells to create human tissue

cartilage: a strong, elastic tissue that connects bones or forms the ears of humans and other animals

dimensions: the measurements or size of an object

Middle Ages: a period in European history from about 500–1500 CE

prototype: the first version of a newly invented object that is tested to see if it will work

stem cell: a human cell that can change into a cell with a specific function

Learn More about 3D Printing

Books

Bodden, Valerie. *3-D Printers*. Minneapolis: Checkerboard Library, 2017. This title takes a closer look at the technology that inspired 3D printing, as well as how it has changed over the years.

Resler, T. J. *How Things Work: Inside Out! Discover Secrets and Science behind Trick Candles, 3D Printers, Penguin Propulsions, and Everything in Between*. Washington, DC: National Geographic Kids, 2017. Instead of taking apart your school's 3D printer to see how it works, read this book! You'll learn about the inner workings of 3D printers and other cool inventions.

Turner, Matt. *Genius Engineering Inventions: From the Plow to 3D Printing*. Minneapolis: Hungry Tomato, 2018. Check out this fun illustrated book about fascinating inventions throughout history.

Websites

Beanz: What Is 3D Printing?
https://www.kidscodecs.com/what-is-3d-printing/
Learn more about how 3D printing works.

Doodle3D
https://www.doodle3d.com
This app turns 2D drawings into 3D designs.

Tinkercad
https://www.tinkercad.com
Try this easy-to-use app to design your own 3D projects.

Index

Photo Acknowledgments

The images in this book are used with the permission of: Alexander Tolstykh/Shutterstock.com, pp. 4, 9; MarinaGrigorivna/Shutterstock.com, pp. 5, 11, 16; Tinxi/Shutterstock.com, pp. 6, 21; NASA/JPL, pp. 7, 26; stockddvideo/Shutterstock.com, p. 8; FabrikaSimf/Shutterstock.com, p. 10; FERNANDO BLANCO CALZADA/Shutterstock.com, p. 12; asharkyu/Shutterstock.com, p. 13; RAGMA IMAGES/Shutterstock.com, p. 14; nikkytok/Shutterstock.com, p. 15; PAUL CROCK/AFP/Getty Images, p. 17; Marco Canoniero/LightRocket/Getty Images, p. 18; Dario Sabljak/Shutterstock.com, p. 19; belekekin/Shutterstock.com, p. 20; Owen Humphreys/PA Images/Getty Images, p. 22; MARY TURNER/REUTERS/Newscom, p. 23; Gennady Grechishkin/Shutterstock.com, p. 24; ESA/Foster + Partners, p. 25; VCG/Getty Images, p. 27; GrashAlex/Shutterstock.com, p. 28; Przemyslaw Szablowski/Shutterstock.com, p. 29.

Front cover: MarinaGrigorivna/Shutterstock.com.